Editor in Chief
Ina Massler Levin, M.A.

Editor
Eric Migliaccio

Contributing Editor
Sarah Smith

Creative Director
Karen J. Goldfluss, M.S. Ed.

Cover Design
Tony Carrillo / Marilyn Goldberg

Teacher Created Resources
12621 Western Avenue
Garden Grove, CA 92841
www.teachercreated.com

ISBN: 978-1-4206-5920-7

Reprinted, 2026
Made in U.S.A.

This book belongs to

____

Ready·Set·Learn

Get Ready to Learn!

Get ready, get set, and go! Boost your child's learning with this exciting series of books. Geared to help children practice and master many needed skills, the *Ready·Set·Learn* books are bursting with 64 pages of learning fun. Use these books for . . .

- enrichment
- skills reinforcement
- extra practice

With their smaller size, the *Ready·Set·Learn* books fit easily in children's hands, backpacks, and book bags. All your child needs to get started are pencils, crayons, and colored pencils.

A full sheet of colorful stickers is included. Use these stickers for . . .

- decorating pages
- rewarding outstanding effort
- keeping track of completed pages

Celebrate your child's progress by using these stickers on the reward chart located on the inside cover. The blue-ribbon sticker fits perfectly on the certificate on page 64.

With *Ready·Set·Learn* and a little encouragement, your child will be on the fast track to learning fun!

Less or More?

Directions: Look at each set. Then write **>** (greater than) or **<** (less than) on the line.

Some numbers are less than other numbers. For example, 4 is less than 5.	Some numbers are greater than other numbers. For example, 5 is greater than 4.
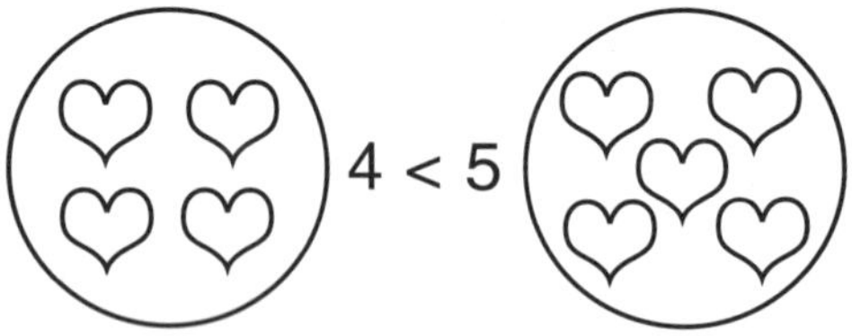	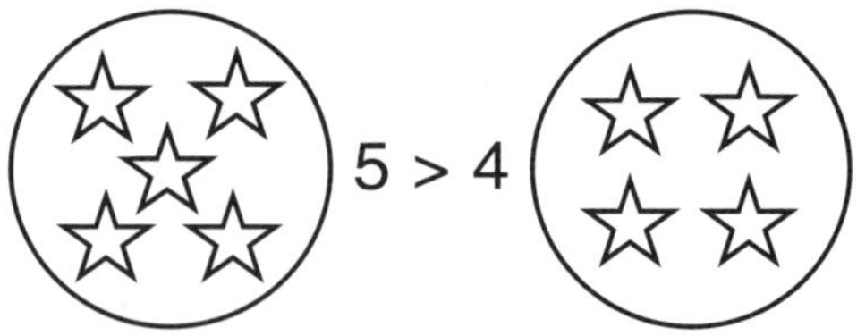

1. 

2. 

3. 

4. 

5. 

Food for Thought

Directions: Circle the set in each row with the *greater* number of vegetables.

1.

2.

Directions: Circle the set in each row with the *smaller* number of fruits.

3.

4.

Hop to It

Directions: Fill in the missing numbers in each row of the bunny's trail.

	2		4		6		8		10		12

		3			6			9			12

1		3			6				10		12

12		10		8		6		4		2	

1			4			7			10		

Gregory the Grasshopper

Directions: Follow Gregory the Grasshopper as he hops along the number line.

1. How many hops did Gregory hop? 6 – 3 = ______

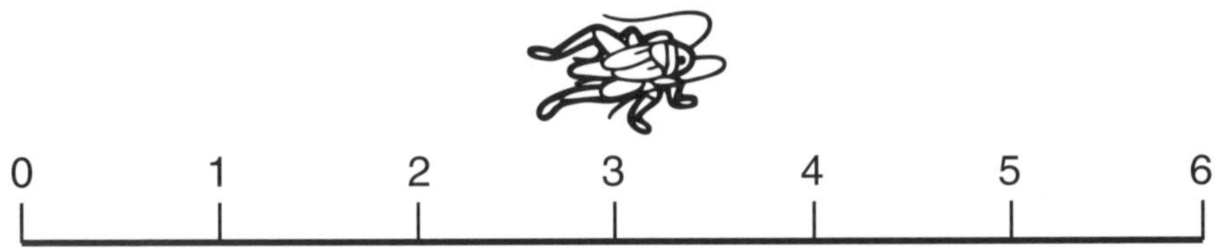

2. How many hops did Gregory hop? 6 – 2 = ______

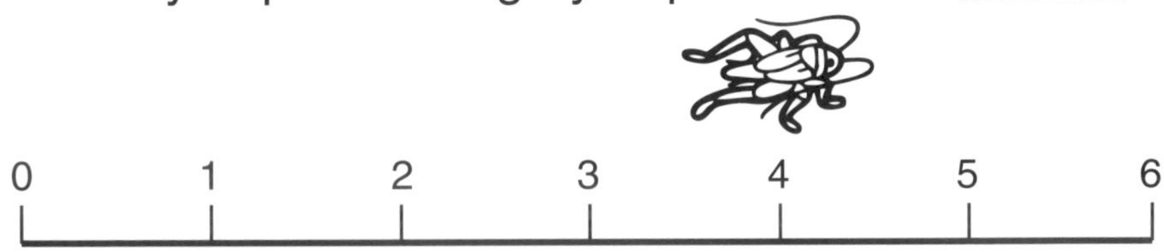

3. How many hops did Gregory hop? 6 – 4 = ______

4. How many hops did Gregory hop? 6 – 5 = ______

Big Shapes, Small Shapes

Directions: Make a ● on the biggest shape in each row. Draw an **X** on the smallest shape in each row.

1.

2.

3.

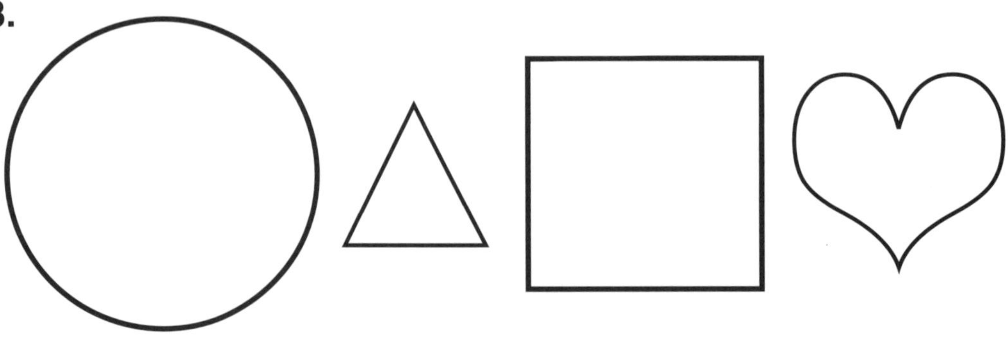

Donut Count

Directions: Count the donuts in each big box and write the number in the smaller box below.

Directions: Look at the numbers below. Draw that number of donuts in each big box.

7	10

Finish the Patterns

Directions: Write the missing number or numbers to complete each pattern.

1.

1	2	3
	5	4

2.

7	8	9	10
	13		11

3.

1	2	3		5
10	9		7	

4.

1	2	1	3		4	1		1

5.

10	11	13	14		17	19		22

6.

1	2		4		6	7		

Ready·Set·Learn

Candy Counting

Directions: Count and add the candy. Write the answer in the box.

A.

2 + 3 = ☐

B.

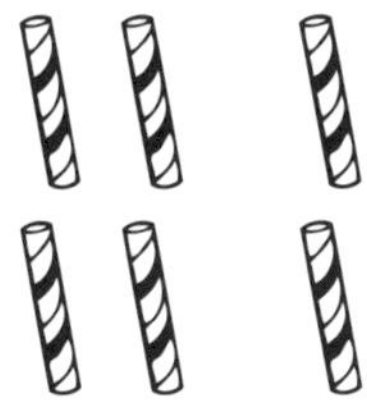

4 + 2 = ☐

C.

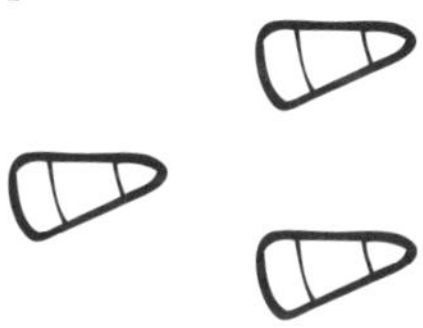

1 + 2 = ☐

D.

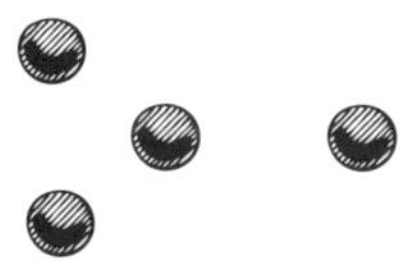

3 + 1 = ☐

E.

4 + 3 = ☐

F.

2 + 2 = ☐

G.

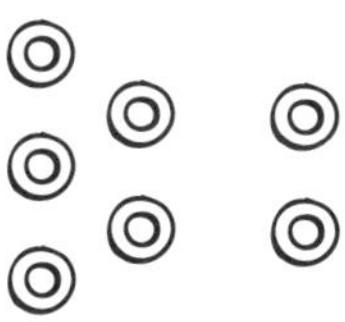

5 + 2 = ☐

H.

3 + 3 = ☐

I.

1 + 1 = ☐

J.

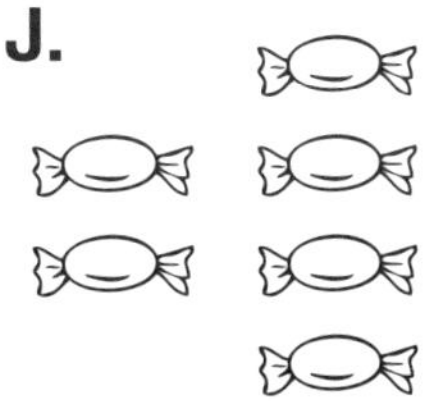

2 + 4 = ☐

How Many Are Left?

Directions: Find out how many are left.

1. Cross out 1 lion.

How many are left? ________

2. Cross out 2 lamps.

How many are left? ________

3. Cross out 5 bugs.

How many are left? ________

4. Cross out 0 spoons.

How many are left? ________

5. Cross out 4 hearts.

How many are left? ________

Complete It!

Directions: Complete each pattern.

1. □ □ △ △ □ □ △ △ ____ ____

2. 3 8 7 4 3 8 7 4 3 8 _____ _____

Directions: Color the circles as shown to continue the pattern.

3. (blue) (yellow) (blue) (yellow) (blue) (yellow) ( ) ( )

4. (red) (green) (green) (red) (green) (green) (red) ( ) ( )

5. (blue) (blue) (red) (red) (red) (blue) (blue) (red) ( ) ( )

6. (blue) (pink) (red) (blue) (pink) (red) (blue) ( ) ( )

Picking Lemons

Directions: "Pick" the lemons on the tree that have number pairs that equal 4. Color them each yellow. Color the lemons that have number pairs that do not equal 4 green.

Animal Match

Directions: Count the animals. Write a number sentence. The first one has been done for you.

1.

4 + 3 = 7

2.

____

3.

____

4.

____

5.

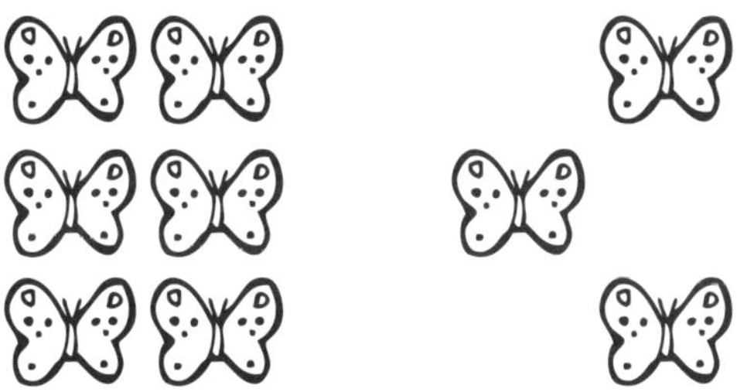

____

6.

____

Add Them Up

Directions: Add the dots on the dice in each row. Write the sum.

1.  + 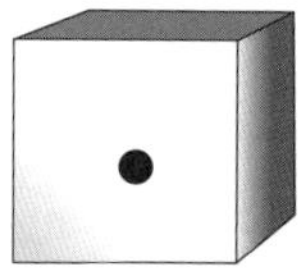 = ____________

2. 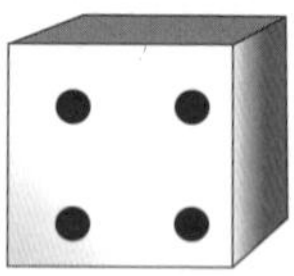 + 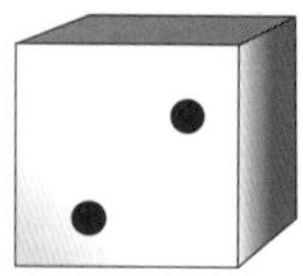 = ____________

3. 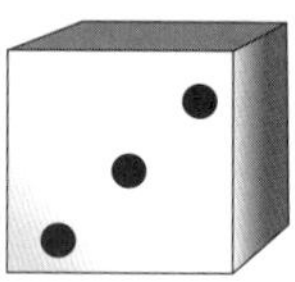 +  = ____________

4. 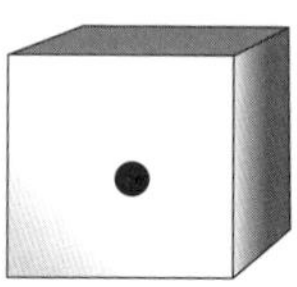 + 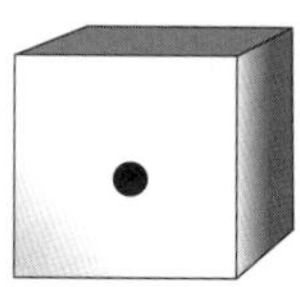 = ____________

5.  +  = ____________

6.  +  = ____________

Cross Out and Subtract

Directions: Solve each problem.

1. Count the cars. Cross out 2 cars. Write the numerals on the lines to show the subtraction problem and answer.

________ – ________ = ________

2. Count the books. Cross out 3 books. Write the numerals on the lines to show the subtraction problem and answer.

________ – ________ = ________

3. Count the fish. Cross out 1 fish. Write the numerals on the lines to show the subtraction problem and answer.

________ – ________ = ________

4. Count the rings. Cross out 2 rings. Write the numerals on the lines to show the subtraction problem and answer.

________ – ________ = ________

Shapely Balloons

Directions: Color the ○s blue. Color the △s green.

Color the □s red.

Lion Tamer

Directions: Help the lion tamer find his lion. Solve the problems. Draw a line from the tamer to the lion with the answer of 3. Color the lion tamer.

Seeking Six

1. Color the fish that have number pairs that equal 6.

2. Color the gifts that have number pairs that equal 6.

3. Color the apples that have number pairs that equal 6.

Crack the Code

Directions: Solve each subtraction problem below. Write the letter that goes with each answer in the box. Use the code to discover the answer.

What did the pebble say to the rock?

E	L	O	R	S	T
1	4	3	0	5	2

$$\begin{array}{r}6\\-2\\\hline\end{array}\quad\begin{array}{r}2\\-1\\\hline\end{array}\quad\begin{array}{r}5\\-3\\\hline\end{array}\quad\begin{array}{r}5\\-0\\\hline\end{array}$$

☐ ☐ ☐ ' ☐

$$\begin{array}{r}4\\-4\\\hline\end{array}\quad\begin{array}{r}6\\-3\\\hline\end{array}\quad\begin{array}{r}5\\-1\\\hline\end{array}\quad\begin{array}{r}4\\-0\\\hline\end{array}$$

☐ ☐ ☐ ☐ !

Shhh! Say It in Code

Directions: Solve each math problem. Write the letter that goes with each answer in the box. Use the code to discover the answer.

What did the camera say to the mouse?

A	C	E	H	S	Y
3	1	5	2	0	4

$\begin{array}{r} 0 \\ +0 \\ \hline \end{array}$ $\begin{array}{r} 2 \\ +1 \\ \hline \end{array}$ $\begin{array}{r} 1 \\ +3 \\ \hline \end{array}$

☐ ☐ ☐

$\begin{array}{r} 1 \\ +0 \\ \hline \end{array}$ $\begin{array}{r} 1 \\ +1 \\ \hline \end{array}$ $\begin{array}{r} 3 \\ +2 \\ \hline \end{array}$ $\begin{array}{r} 4 \\ +1 \\ \hline \end{array}$ $\begin{array}{r} 0 \\ +0 \\ \hline \end{array}$ $\begin{array}{r} 5 \\ +0 \\ \hline \end{array}$

☐ ☐ ☐ ☐ ☐ ☐!

Butterfly Addition

Directions: Cross out each answer in the net as you solve the problems.

Hole in One

Directions: Find the answer to each problem. Write your answer on the line below each hole.

A. 9 – 6 = __________

B. 8 – 6 = __________

C. 9 – 8 = __________

D. 9 – 5 = __________

E. 8 – 3 = __________

F. 9 – 3 = __________

G. 9 – 0 = __________

H. 9 – 1 = __________

I. 9 – 2 = __________

What Came First?

Directions: Look at each row of pictures below. They tell a story, but it is not in order. Put the story in order. Write **1**, **2**, or **3** under each picture.

1. 

______ ______ ______

2. 

______ ______ ______

3. 

______ ______ ______

Addition Word Problems

Directions: Solve each problem. Write a number sentence to show your answer.

1.

Sue counted 8 red roses and 6 white roses in the garden. How many roses did Sue find in all?

____

2.

Dan ate 3 apples for breakfast. He ate 4 more for snack. How many apples did he eat in all?

____

3.

My mom bought 4 pizzas. My dad bought 5 pizzas. How many pizzas did they buy in all?

____

4.

Joe saw 9 butterflies. Jack saw 3 butterflies. How many butterflies did they see in all?

____

5.

Alex made 7 books using crayons and 4 books using markers. How many books did he make in all?

____

6.

My aunt baked 5 hams. My grandpa baked 5 hams. How many hams did they bake in all?

____

Addition

Directions: Add the numbers together.

A.
$$\begin{array}{r} 1 \\ +\ 8 \\ \hline \end{array}$$

B.
$$\begin{array}{r} 5 \\ +\ 5 \\ \hline \end{array}$$

C.
$$\begin{array}{r} 2 \\ +\ 6 \\ \hline \end{array}$$

D.
$$\begin{array}{r} 9 \\ +\ 0 \\ \hline \end{array}$$

E.
$$\begin{array}{r} 7 \\ +\ 1 \\ \hline \end{array}$$

F.
$$\begin{array}{r} 4 \\ +\ 7 \\ \hline \end{array}$$

G.
$$\begin{array}{r} 10 \\ +\ 2 \\ \hline \end{array}$$

H.
$$\begin{array}{r} 3 \\ +\ 8 \\ \hline \end{array}$$

I.
$$\begin{array}{r} 8 \\ +\ 3 \\ \hline \end{array}$$

Shoes and Socks

Directions: Draw a line to match each equation to its answer.

1. 8 – 3 = _____
2. 2 – 1 = _____
3. 7 – 5 = _____
4. 6 – 2 = _____
5. 10 – 3 = _____

7

2

1

5

4

Subtraction

Directions: Solve each problem.

A. $\begin{array}{r} 5 \\ -\ 4 \\ \hline \end{array}$

B. $\begin{array}{r} 6 \\ -\ 3 \\ \hline \end{array}$

C. $\begin{array}{r} 7 \\ -\ 5 \\ \hline \end{array}$

D. $\begin{array}{r} 10 \\ -\ 6 \\ \hline \end{array}$

E. $\begin{array}{r} 9 \\ -\ 2 \\ \hline \end{array}$

F. $\begin{array}{r} 8 \\ -\ 1 \\ \hline \end{array}$

G. $\begin{array}{r} 7 \\ -\ 4 \\ \hline \end{array}$

H. $\begin{array}{r} 3 \\ -\ 2 \\ \hline \end{array}$

I. $\begin{array}{r} 4 \\ -\ 0 \\ \hline \end{array}$

Subtraction Action

Directions: Solve each problem. Write the number sentence.

1.

Jim had 9 oranges. He ate 2. How many are left?

____

2.

Jake had 8 candy bars. His friend ate 2 of them. How many candy bars does Jake have left?

____

3.

Deb had 5 dolls. Now she only has 2. How many dolls did she lose?

____

4.

Lisa has a cat with 6 fleas. If 3 jumped off, how many fleas are left?

____

5.

Hope picked 7 strawberries. John ate 4 of them. How many does Hope have left?

____

6.

Ken found 4 snails in the garden. He picked up 2 of them. How many snails are left in the garden?

____

Add It Up

Directions: Find the sums to the addition problems below.

1. 1 + 3 = ____________

2. 5 + 8 = ____________

3. 3 + 7 = ____________

4. 9 + 3 = ____________

5. 6 + 1 = ____________

6. 2 + 4 = ____________

7. 1 + 2 = ____________

8. 8 + 0 = ____________

9. 0 + 3 = ____________

10. 4 + 6 = ____________

11. 7 + 7 = ____________

12. 3 + 5 = ____________

13. 4 + 2 = ____________

14. 9 + 2 = ____________

15. 6 + 9 = ____________

16. 3 + 2 = ____________

17. 2 + 0 = ____________

18. 6 + 2 = ____________

19. 9 + 5 = ____________

20. 1 + 6 = ____________

Find the Differences

Directions: Find the differences. Color the picture.

2 = green	3 = orange	4 = brown	5 = blue	6 = yellow

GREAT
#1
YEAH!
COOL
WOW
NEAT
NEAT
GREAT
YEAH!
#1
GREAT
SUPER
WOW
YEAH!
#1
TOPS
SUPER
#1

#1
GREAT
YEAH!
WOW
GREAT
YEAH!
WOW
COOL
YEAH!
TOPS
TOPS
SUPER

Add It!

Directions: Solve the problems below.

1.	2.	3.	4.	5.
6 + 2 = ___	3 + 8 = ___	4 + 7 = ___	7 + 0 = ___	5 + 4 = ___
6.	**7.**	**8.**	**9.**	**10.**
2 + 7 = ___	0 + 9 = ___	6 + 4 = ___	8 + 1 = ___	10 + 2 = ___

11.	12.
7 + 4 = ____________	1 + 7 = ____________
13.	**14.**
9 + 3 = ____________	10 + 1 = ____________

Subtract It!

Directions: Solve the problems below.

1. 7 – 3 ____	2. 9 – 7 ____	3. 6 – 5 ____	4. 5 – 4 ____	5. 10 – 5 ____
6. 8 – 4 ____	7. 4 – 2 ____	8. 2 – 1 ____	9. 3 – 3 ____	10. 6 – 3 ____

11. $9 - 9 =$ ________	12. $7 - 4 =$ ________
13. $12 - 6 =$ ________	14. $8 - 5 =$ ________

Make the Sentence

Directions: Read each word problem. Create the correct number sentence for each problem.

1. Five birds sat on a fence. Two birds flew away. How many birds were left?

☐ – ☐ = ☐

2. Seven kids were swimming in a pool. Three kids got out of the pool. How many kids were left?

☐ – ☐ = ☐

3. Three boys were riding their bikes. All of the boys had to go home. How many boys were left?

☐ – ☐ = ☐

4. Mom had six cookies. She gave two cookies to me. Now how many cookies does mom have?

☐ – ☐ = ☐

5. I had nine flowers in the garden. I picked five flowers to bring in the house. Now how many flowers are in the garden?

☐ – ☐ = ☐

6. Mark had four apples. He ate one apple every day for three days. How many apples does he have left?

☐ – ☐ = ☐

Nifty Fifty

Directions: Count to fifty.

1. Can you count to 50 by twos? Fill in the missing numbers.

2, 4, 6, ________ , 10, 12, ________ , 16,
18, ________ , 22, ________ , 26, 28, 30,
________ , 34, 36, ________ , ________ ,
42, 44, ________ , 48, ________

2. Can you count to 50 by fives? Fill in the missing numbers.

5, 10, ________ , 20, ________ , ________ ,
35, 40, 45, ________

3. Can you count to 50 by tens? Fill in the missing numbers.

10, ________ , 30, ________ , 50

Working with Pennies

Directions: Color in the pennies to show how much each item costs.

1.  5¢ — 1¢ 1¢ 1¢ 1¢ 1¢ 1¢ 1¢ 1¢ 1¢ 1¢

2.  2¢ — 1¢ 1¢ 1¢ 1¢ 1¢ 1¢ 1¢ 1¢ 1¢ 1¢

3.  7¢ — 1¢ 1¢ 1¢ 1¢ 1¢ 1¢ 1¢ 1¢ 1¢ 1¢

4. 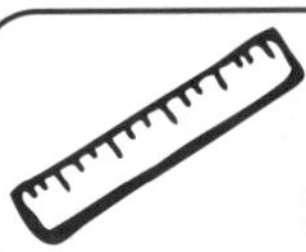 6¢ — 1¢ 1¢ 1¢ 1¢ 1¢ 1¢ 1¢ 1¢ 1¢ 1¢

5.  3¢ — 1¢ 1¢ 1¢ 1¢ 1¢ 1¢ 1¢ 1¢ 1¢ 1¢

6. 

8¢ — 1¢ 1¢ 1¢ 1¢ 1¢ 1¢ 1¢ 1¢ 1¢ 1¢

7. 

10¢ — 1¢ 1¢ 1¢ 1¢ 1¢ 1¢ 1¢ 1¢ 1¢ 1¢

8. 

1¢ — 1¢ 1¢ 1¢ 1¢ 1¢ 1¢ 1¢ 1¢ 1¢ 1¢

Coin Purses

Directions: Count the coins in each purse. Write the total amount of money on the line.

1.

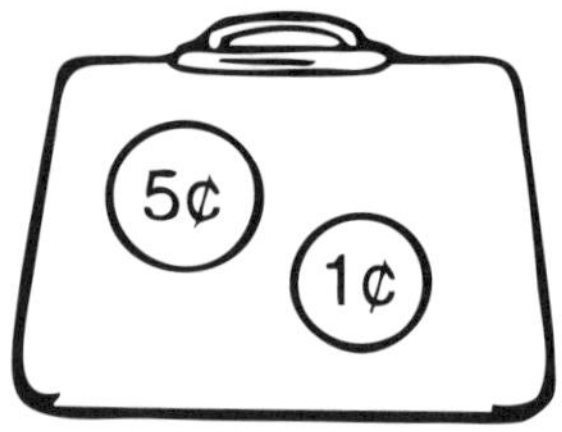

_______ ¢

2.

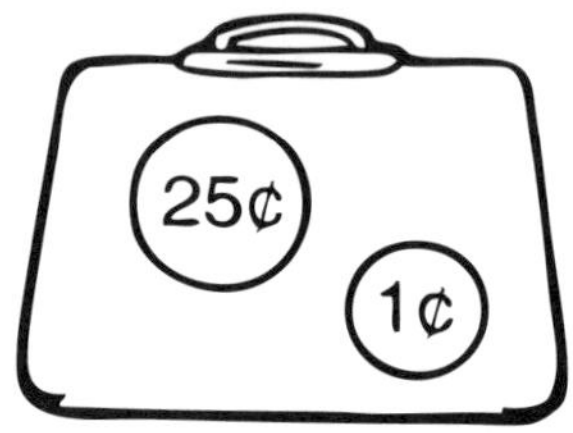

_______ ¢

3.

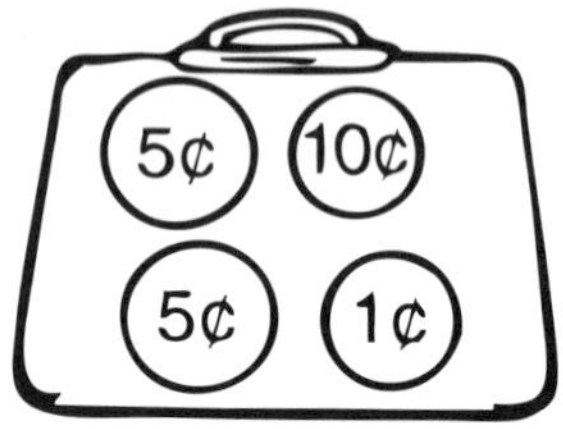

_______ ¢

4.

_______ ¢

5.

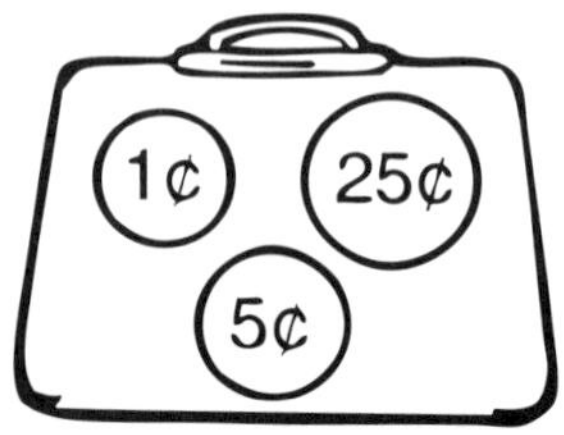

_______ ¢

6.

_______ ¢

7.

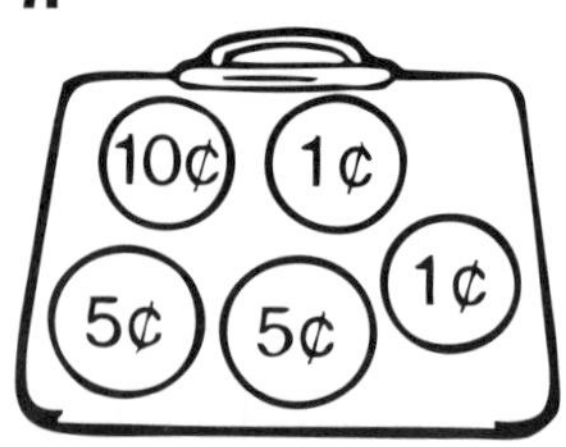

_______ ¢

8.

_______ ¢

Ready·Set·Learn

Odd or Even

Directions: Look at the number in each box. Decide if it is *odd* or *even*. Circle the correct word.

1.	2.	3.	4.	5.	6.
2	13	4	8	9	20
odd even	odd even	odd even	odd even	odd even	odd even
7.	8.	9.	10.	11.	12.
17	12	15	16	6	1
odd even	odd even	odd even	odd even	odd even	odd even

Directions: Color the *even* numbers *yellow*. Color the *odd* numbers *blue*. Find the hidden number.

2	90	38	46	88	12	92	44	68
92	3	22	23	66	17	87	1	4
56	15	98	11	36	45	16	91	24
58	57	39	75	6	27	59	73	54
8	72	50	29	62	78	100	69	10
40	48	26	47	14	32	52	37	48
18	96	70	96	86	38	20	42	80

The *hidden* number is _______________.

Sundae Surprise

Directions: Solve the problems. Color the scoops like this:

7 = brown	*8 = white*	*9 = pink*

Numbers Large and Small

Directions: Circle the **greater** number.

1. 19 13	2. 73 81	3. 24 21	4. 37 26	5. 62 78
6. 53 58	7. 38 28	8. 45 49	9. 10 15	10. 85 90

Directions: Circle the **lesser** number.

11. 17 21	12. 47 32	13. 58 51	14. 75 79	15. 80 91
16. 33 27	17. 66 56	18. 81 88	19. 37 43	20. 16 26

Add and Subtract

Directions: Fill in the circle under the number that completes each math sentence.

1.	**2.**	**3.**
6 + _______ = 10 3 ○ 4 ○ 5 ○ 6 ○	2 + _______ = 9 6 ○ 7 ○ 8 ○ 9 ○	10 + _______ = 10 0 ○ 1 ○ 2 ○ 3 ○
4.	**5.**	**6.**
1 + _______ = 5 1 ○ 2 ○ 3 ○ 4 ○	8 + _______ = 10 0 ○ 1 ○ 2 ○ 3 ○	2 + _______ = 8 3 ○ 4 ○ 5 ○ 6 ○
7.	**8.**	**9.**
10 – _______ = 7 0 ○ 1 ○ 2 ○ 3 ○	10 – _______ = 1 6 ○ 7 ○ 8 ○ 9 ○	7 – _______ = 2 5 ○ 6 ○ 7 ○ 8 ○
10.	**11.**	**12.**
6 – _______ = 1 3 ○ 4 ○ 5 ○ 6 ○	7 – _______ = 4 3 ○ 4 ○ 5 ○ 6 ○	9 – _______ = 4 4 ○ 5 ○ 6 ○ 7 ○

Number Words

Directions: Write the number word below each number. Use the words in the word box.

eighteen	two	four	seven
zero	one	three	nine
six	five	ten	twelve
twenty-five	fifteen	twenty-two	

a. 6 ____________	**b.** 9 ____________	**c.** 0 ____________
d. 3 ____________	**e.** 18 ____________	**f.** 7 ____________
g. 1 ____________	**h.** 25 ____________	**i.** 2 ____________
j. 4 ____________	**k.** 10 ____________	**l.** 12 ____________
m. 15 ____________	**n.** 22 ____________	**o.** 5 ____________

Ready·Set·Learn

Before and After

Directions: Write the number that comes before and after each number on the shirts.

1. ____ **91** ____

2. ____ **60** ____

3. ____ **70** ____

4. ____ **33** ____

5. ____ **17** ____

6. ____ **48** ____

7. ____ **25** ____

8. ____ **59** ____

9. ____ **29** ____

Writing Fact Families

Directions: Use the numbers in each cloud to write a **fact family**. The first one has been done for you.

1. 2, 3, 5

2 + 3 = 5

3 + 2 = 5

5 – 3 = 2

5 – 2 = 3

2. 4, 5, 9

3. 1, 2, 3

4. 7, 2, 9

5. 3, 5, 8

6. 1, 8, 9

7. 4, 2, 6

8. 3, 4, 7

9. 6, 3, 9

Market Street Math

Directions: You have just 85 cents to spend on Market Street. You are allowed to buy any two items from the choices below. Can you find two items that you could buy for 85 cents or less? Think of as many combinations of two items as you can. Write the combinations and the cost on the lines below. (An example has been done for you.)

 milk = 65¢	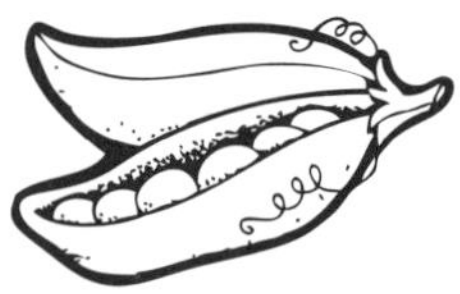 peas = 25¢	 cereal = 70¢
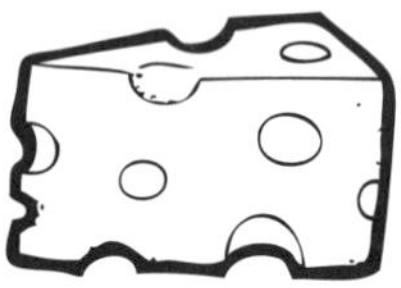 cheese = 60¢	 apple = 15¢	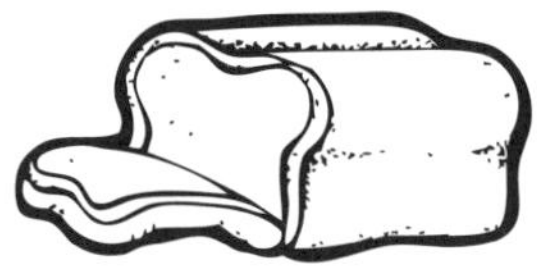 bread = 55¢
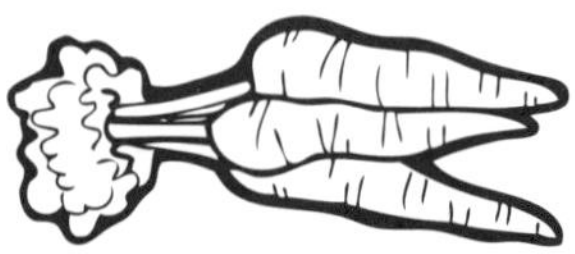 carrots = 20¢	 hot dog = 30¢	 peaches = 20¢

peas (25¢) + bread (55¢) = 80¢

__________ + __________ = ______

__________ + __________ = ______

__________ + __________ = ______

__________ + __________ = ______

__________ + __________ = ______

Numbers Gone Wild!

Directions: The runners from the race got mixed up. Can you put their numbers back in order so the race can start? Order them from the smallest number to the greatest. Write your answers on the lines below.

1. ______________________ **5.** ______________________

2. ______________________ **6.** ______________________

3. ______________________ **7.** ______________________

4. ______________________

Time for Fun

Directions: Color the round clock that shows the digital clock's time.

1.

2.

3.

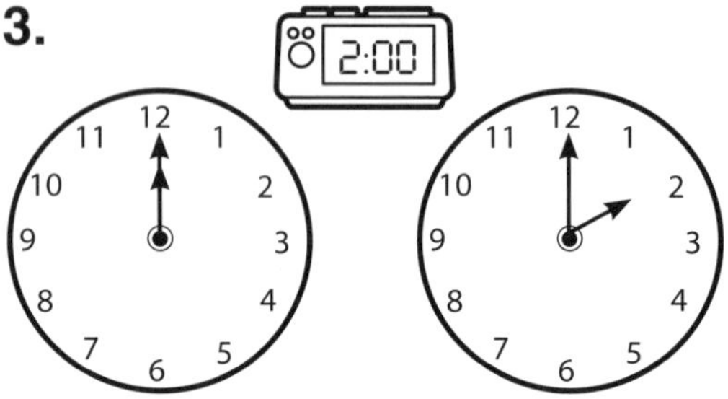

4.

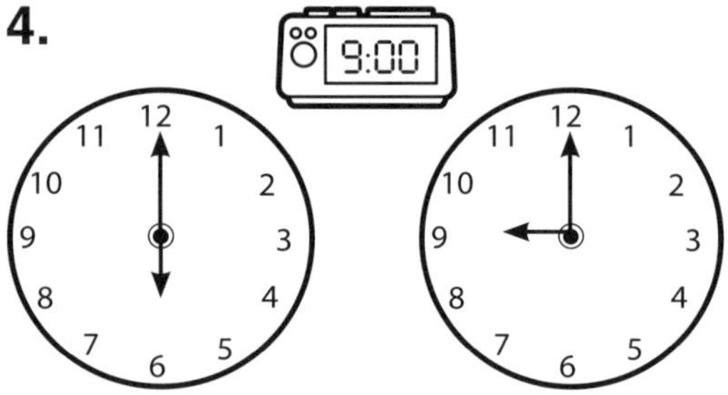

5.

6.

7.

8.

Sets of Five

Directions: Color every set of five stars or planets.

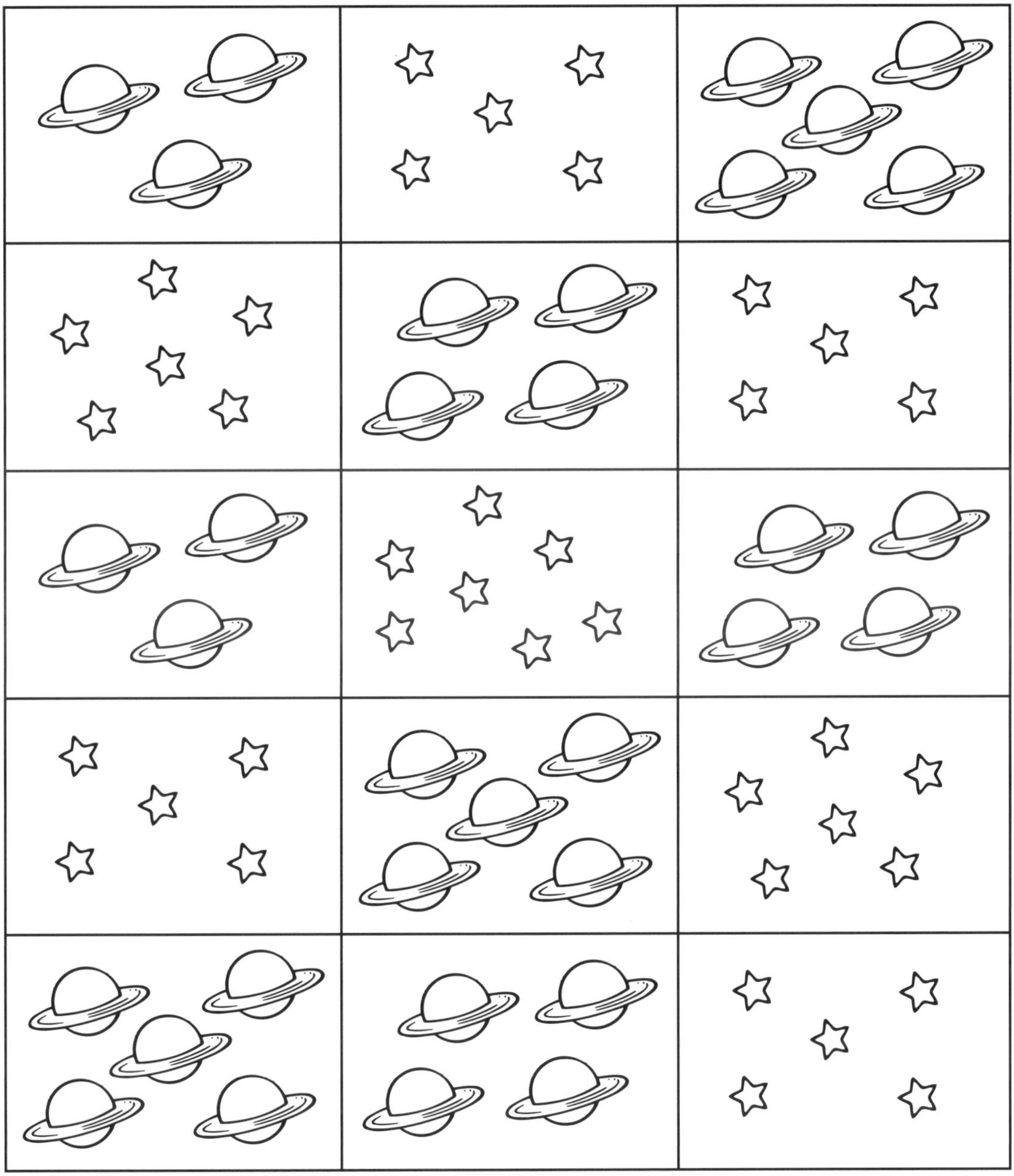

Make a Number

Directions: Use the two numbers shown to make new numbers. Make the largest number and the smallest number. The first one has been done for you.

1. 5, 2 — Largest 52, Smallest 25	**2.** 9, 5 — Largest ____, Smallest ____	**3.** 3, 6 — Largest ____, Smallest ____
4. 7, 5 — Largest ____, Smallest ____	**5.** 4, 8 — Largest ____, Smallest ____	**6.** 6, 9 — Largest ____, Smallest ____
7. 1, 7 — Largest ____, Smallest ____	**8.** 3, 4 — Largest ____, Smallest ____	**9.** 7, 9 — Largest ____, Smallest ____
10. 8, 2 — Largest ____, Smallest ____	**11.** 6, 4 — Largest ____, Smallest ____	**12.** 1, 8 — Largest ____, Smallest ____

Add It!

Directions: Solve by writing out the complete addition sentence. At the bottom of the page, answer each problem.

1. Krysten has 5 books. Zoe has 10 books. How many books do they have in all? _____ + _____ = _____ books	**2.** Leanne has 9 pennies. She finds 6 more pennies. How many pennies does she have in all? _____ + _____ = _____ pennies
3. Bruce and Stan have 10 toy cars. They buy 2 more toy cars. How many toy cars do they have in all? _____ + _____ = _____ toy cars	**4.** Vickie has 6 roses. Michelle has 6 roses. How many roses do they have in all? _____ + _____ = _____ roses

5. $6 + 8$ ____

6. $5 + 9$ ____

7. $8 + 3$ ____

8. $6 + 6$ ____

9. $2 + 9$ ____

10. $9 + 8$ ____

11. $10 + 5$ ____

12. $9 + 4$ ____

13. $8 + 8$ ____

14. $4 + 7$ ____

Missing Apartment Numbers

Directions: Fill in the missing apartment numbers.

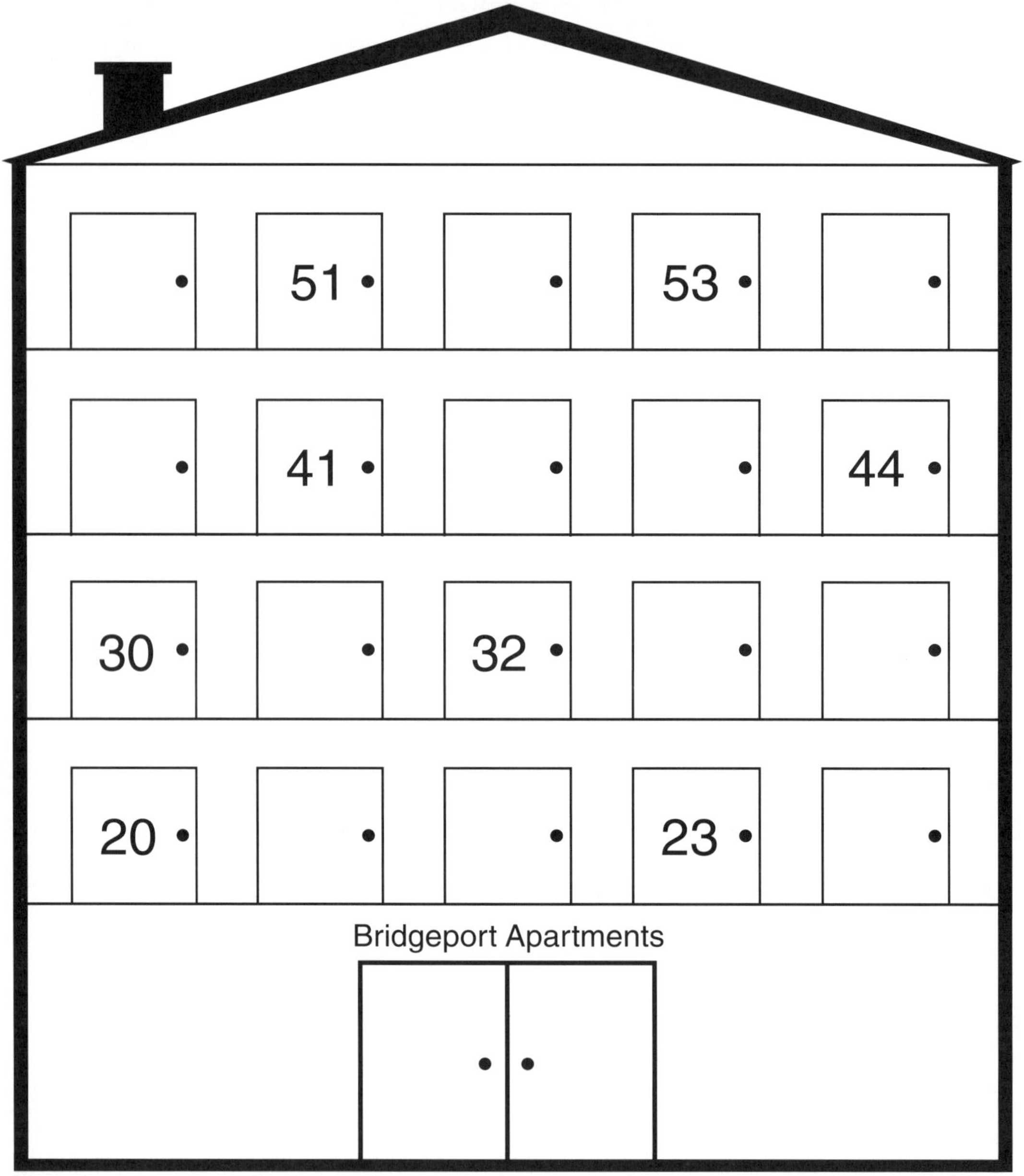

"Sweet" Word Problems

Directions: Give the answer for each word problem.

1.

Timmy ate 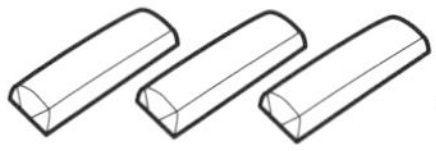.

Billy ate 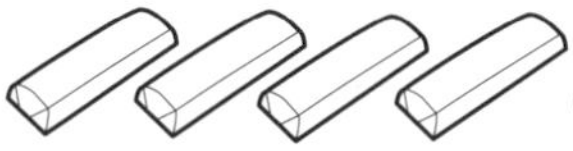.

How many candy bars did they eat in all? ________________

2.

Juan bought  on Monday.

On Wednesday, he bought  more.

How many cookies did he buy in all? ________________

3.

Tina had 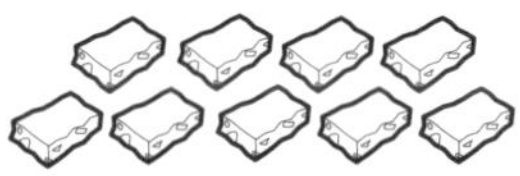.

She gave 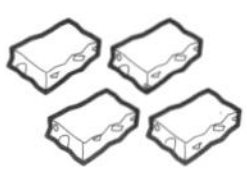 to her friend.

How many brownies did she have left? ________________

4.

Antonio had 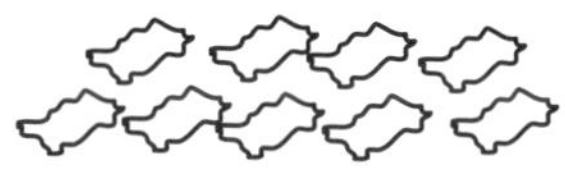.

He found 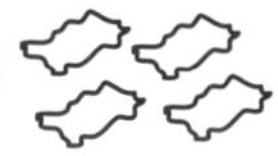 more.

How many candy wrappers did he have in all? ________________

5.

There were  in a bag.

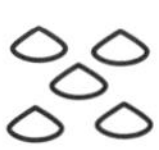 were eaten at recess.

How many chocolate chips were left? ________________

6.

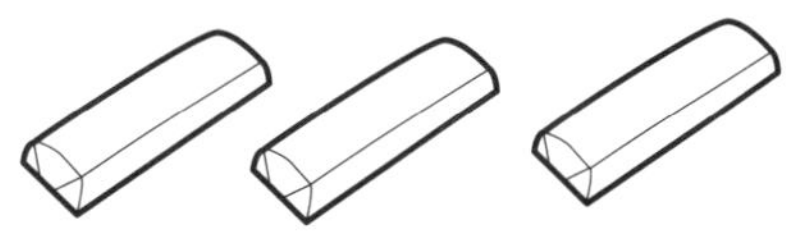

How many more cupcakes are there than candy bars?

____

What's the Sign?

Directions: Use <, >, or = to complete each number sentence.

>	greater than
<	less than
=	equal to

1. 6 ________ 16	**2.** 90 ________ 9	**3.** 5 ________ 37
4. 10 ________ 10	**5.** 19 ________ 11	**6.** 51 ________ 31
7. 23 ________ 32	**8.** 20 ________ 20	**9.** 76 ________ 56
10. 86 ________ 86	**11.** 2 ________ 11	**12.** 14 ________ 29

More Time for Fun

Directions: Color the digital clock that shows the correct time.

1.

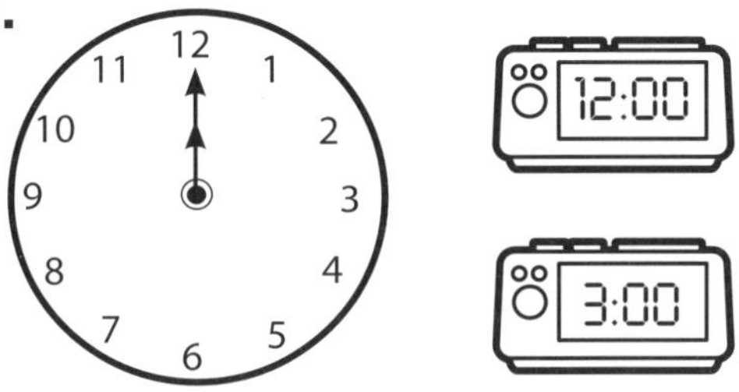

2.

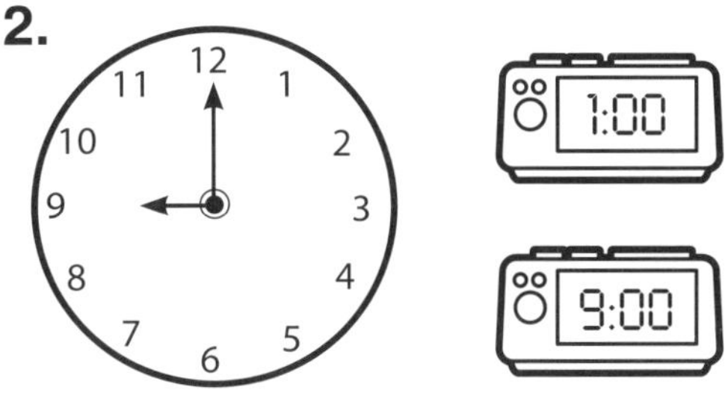

3.

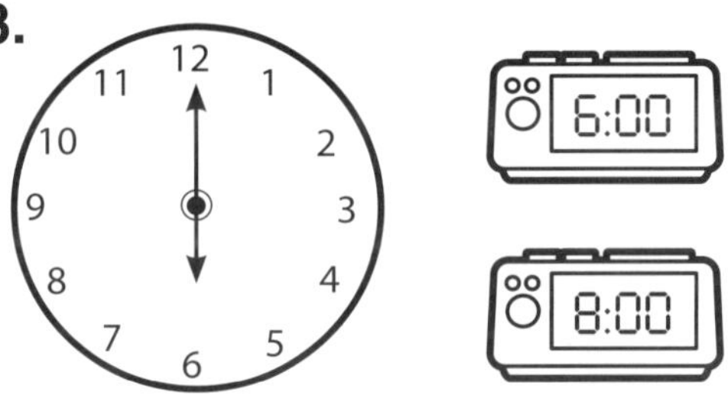

4.

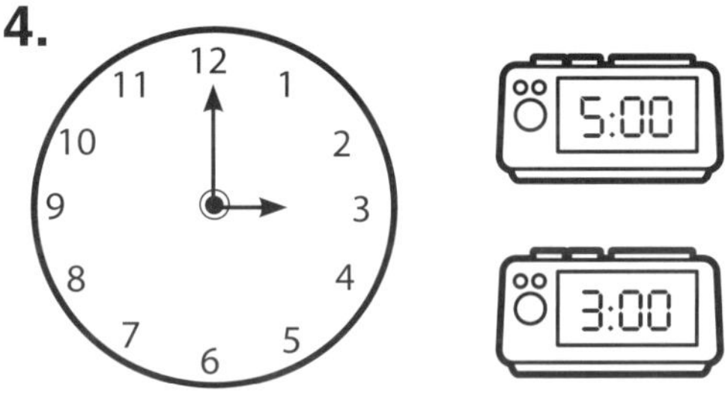

5.

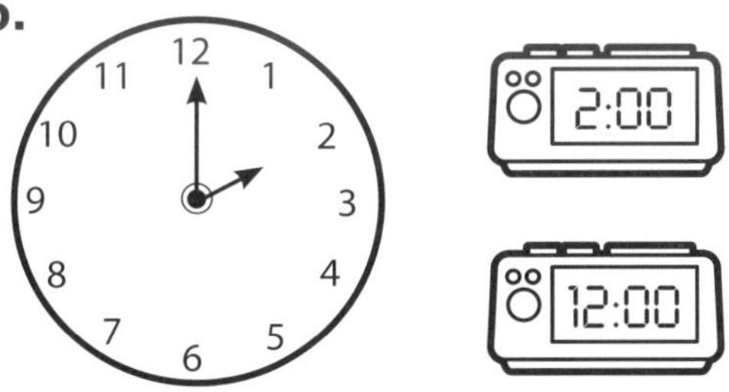

6.

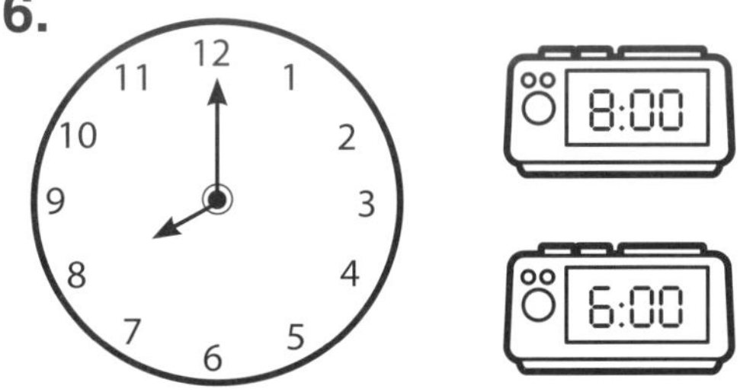

7.

8.

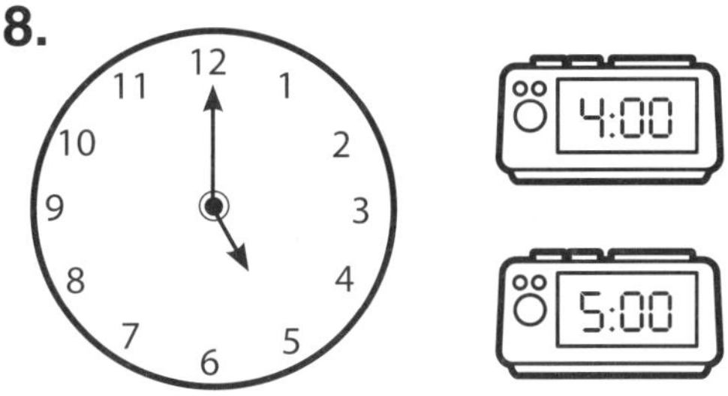

Find the Numbers

Directions: Use the clues to circle the correct number or numbers.

1. Circle the numbers that have a **4** in the **tens** place.

   43 29 63 41 78 37 49

2. Circle the numbers that have a **9** in the **ones** place.

   19 97 58 79 63 9 29

3. Circle the number that has **2 tens** and **5 ones**.

   35 57 52 26 25 53 16

4. Circle the numbers that have a **zero** in the **ones** place.

   21 60 43 30 76 43 75

5. Circle the numbers that have **nothing** in the **tens** place.

   43 7 17 8 2 59 36

6. Circle the number that has a **1** in the **hundreds** place.

   10 61 100 43 90 82 41

What's the Time?

Directions: Write the time that each clock shows.

1. ______________

2. ______________

3. ______________

4. ______________

5. ______________

6. ______________

7. ______________

8. ______________

9. ______________

Mystery Numbers

Directions: Follow the directions below to make a number.

1. Make a number that has . . .
a **two** in the **ones** place,
a **five** in the **tens** place,
a **nine** in the **hundreds** place.

hundreds	tens	ones

2. Make a number that has . . .
a **six** in the **ones** place,
an **eight** in the **tens** place,
a **one** in the **hundreds** place.

hundreds	tens	ones

3. Make a number that has . . .
a **three** in the **ones** place,
a **zero** in the **tens** place,
a **four** in the **hundreds** place.

hundreds	tens	ones

4. Make a number that has . . .
a **seven** in the **ones** place,
a **six** in the **tens** place,
a **two** in the **hundreds** place.

hundreds	tens	ones

5. Make a number that has . . .
an **eight** in the **ones** place,
a **nine** in the **tens** place,
a **three** in the **hundreds** place.

hundreds	tens	ones

Ordinal Numbers

Directions: Draw a line to match the ordinal number to its medal. The first one is done for you.

3rd	fifth	8th
	second	
7th	first	2nd
	seventh	
4th	tenth	10th
	third	
9th	sixth	5th
	ninth	
1st	fourth	6th
	eighth	

Equal Parts

Directions: Read each word problem. Divide the shape or circle the fraction to show the answer.

1. Jenni and Drew want to share a candy bar. Draw a line to show how Jenni and Drew will get equal amounts of the candy bar.

2. George, Angie, and Nicky want to equally share a small, round pizza. Circle the fraction that shows what part each one will get.

$\frac{1}{2}$ $\frac{1}{4}$ $\frac{1}{3}$

3. Kyle and Terri have a bag of jellybeans. How much of the bag will each get if they want the same amount of jellybeans?

$\frac{1}{2}$ $\frac{1}{4}$ $\frac{1}{3}$

4. Sophia and Maria want to share a sandwich. Draw a line on the sandwich to show how they will get equal parts of the sandwich.

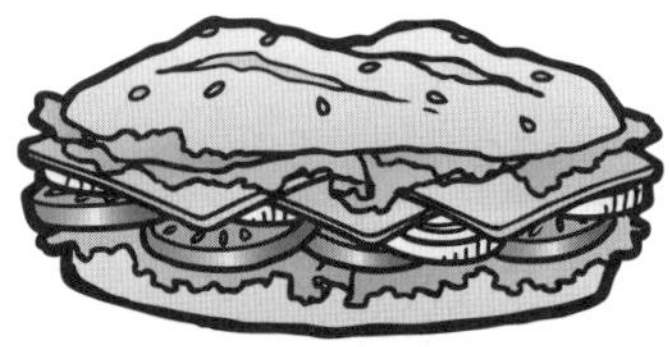

5. Mrs. Long and her three children want to share a pizza. Divide the pizza into 4 equal parts so that they all get the same amount.

6. Judy and her mom and dad want to share a chocolate bar. Draw lines to show how Judy, her mom, and her dad will get equal parts of the chocolate bar.

Answer Key

Page 4
1. >
2. >
3. <
4. >
5. <

Page 5
1. circle 2nd set
2. circle 1st set
3. circle 1st set
4. circle 2nd set

Page 6
First row: 1, 3, 5, 7, 9, 11
Second row: 1, 2, 4, 5, 7, 8, 10, 11
Third row: 2, 4, 5, 7, 8, 9, 11
Fourth row: 11, 9, 7, 5, 3, 1
Fifth row: 2, 3, 5, 6, 8, 9, 11, 12

Page 7
1. 3
2. 4
3. 2
4. 1

Page 9
9, 5, 8

Page 10
1. 6
2. 14, 12
3. 4, 8, 6
4. 1, 5
5. 16, 20
6. 3, 5, 8, 9

Page 11
A. 5
B. 6
C. 3
D. 4
E. 7
F. 4
G. 7
H. 6
I. 2
J. 6

Page 12
1. 6
2 4
3. 3
4. 6
5. 5

Page 13
1. □ □
2. 7, 4
3. blue, yellow
4. green, green
5. red, red
6. pink, red

Page 14
Check students' addition problems.

Page 15
2. 3 + 5 = 8
3. 2 + 4 = 6
4. 5 + 5 = 10
5. 6 + 3 = 9
6. 4 + 1 = 5

Page 16
1. 7
2. 6
3. 8
4. 2
5. 5
6. 4

Page 17
1. 6 – 2 = 4
2. 7 – 3 = 4
3. 9 – 1 = 8
4. 3 – 2 = 1

Page 19
3 – 2 = 1
7 – 2 = 5
5 – 2 = 3
6 – 5 = 1
4 – 4 = 0
6 – 4 = 2

Page 20
1. 6, 8, 6, 6
2. 6, 4, 3, 6
3. 5, 6, 6, 5

Page 21
6 – 2 = 4, 2 – 1 = 1
5 – 3 = 2, 5 – 0 = 5
4 – 4 = 0, 6 – 3 = 3
5 – 1 = 4, 4 – 0 = 4
Answer: Let's roll!

Page 22
0 + 0 = 0, 2 + 1 = 3
1 + 3 = 4, 1 + 0 = 1
1 + 1 = 2, 3 + 2 = 5
4 + 1 = 5, 0 + 0 = 0
5 + 0 = 5
Answer: Say cheese!

Page 23
5, 8, 11
6, 15, 13
10, 16, 15

Page 24
A. 3
B. 2
C. 1
D. 4
E. 5
F. 6
G. 9
H. 8
I. 7

Page 25
1. 3, 1, 2
2. 3, 2, 1
3. 2, 1, 3

Page 26
1. 8 + 6 = 14 roses
2. 3 + 4 = 7 apples
3. 4 + 5 = 9 pizzas
4. 9 + 3 = 12 butterflies
5. 7 + 4 = 11 books
6. 5 + 5 = 10 hams

Page 27
A. 9
B. 10
C. 8
D. 9
E. 8
F. 11
G. 12
H. 11
I. 11

Page 28
1. 8 – 3 = 5
2. 2 – 1 = 1
3. 7 – 5 = 2
4. 6 – 2 = 4
5. 10 – 3 = 7

Page 29
A. 1
B. 3
C. 2
D. 4
E. 7
F. 7
G. 3
H. 1
I. 4

Page 30
1. 9 – 2 = 7 oranges
2. 8 – 2 = 6 candy bars
3. 5 – 2 = 3 dolls
4. 6 – 3 = 3 fleas
5. 7 – 4 = 3 strawberries
6. 4 – 2 = 2 snails

Page 31
1. 4
2. 13
3. 10
4. 12
5. 7
6. 6
7. 3
8. 8
9. 3
10. 10
11. 14
12. 8
13. 6
14. 11
15. 15
16. 5
17. 2
18. 8
19. 14
20. 7

Page 32
1. 5 – 1 = 4, brown
2. 6 – 2 = 4, brown
3. 9 – 3 = 6, yellow
4. 10 – 7 = 3, orange
5. 5 – 0 = 5, blue
6. 3 – 1 = 2, green
7. 7 – 1 = 6, yellow
8. 9 – 6 = 3, orange
9. 8 – 2 = 6, yellow
10. 6 – 4 = 2, green

Page 33
1. 8
2. 11
3. 11
4. 7
5. 9
6. 9
7. 9
8. 10
9. 9
10. 12
11. 11
12. 8
13. 12
14. 11

Page 34
1. 4
2. 2
3. 1
4. 1
5. 5
6. 4
7. 2
8. 1
9. 0
10. 3
11. 0
12. 3
13. 6
14. 3

Page 35
1. 5 – 2 = 3
2. 7 – 3 = 4
3. 3 – 3 = 0
4. 6 – 2 = 4
5. 9 – 5 = 4
6. 4 – 3 = 1

Page 36
1. 8, 14, 20, 24, 32, 38, 40, 46, 50
2. 15, 25, 30, 50
3. 20, 40

Page 37
1. color in 5 pennies
2. color in 2 pennies
3. color in 7 pennies
4. color in 6 pennies
5. color in 3 pennies
6. color in 8 pennies
7. color in 10 pennies
8. color in 1 penny

Page 38
1. 6¢
2. 26¢
3. 21¢
4. 38¢
5. 31¢
6. 41¢
7. 22¢
8. 31¢

Answer Key

Page 39
1. even
2. odd
3. even
4. even
5. odd
6. even
7. odd
8. even
9. odd
10. even
11. even
12. odd

Hidden number: 49

Page 40
9 – pink, 7 – brown
8 – white, 7 – brown,
8 – white
8 – white, 9 – pink,
7 – brown, 8 – white
9 – pink, 9 – pink, 9 – pink,
8 – white, 9 – pink
7 – brown, 8 – white,
7 – brown, 9 – pink,
7 – brown, 7 – brown

Page 41
1. 19
2. 81
3. 24
4. 37
5. 78
6. 58
7. 38
8. 49
9. 15
10. 90
11. 17
12. 32
13. 51
14. 75
15. 80
16. 27
17. 56
18. 81
19. 37
20. 16

Page 42
1. 4
2. 7
3. 0
4. 4
5. 2
6. 6
7. 3
8. 9
9. 5
10. 5
11. 3
12. 5

Page 43
a. six
b. nine
c. zero
d. three
e. eighteen
f. seven
g. one
h. twenty–five
i. two
j. four
k. ten
l. twelve
m. fifteen
n. twenty–two
o. five

Page 44
1. 90, 92
2. 59, 61
3. 69, 71
4. 32, 34
5. 16, 18
6. 47, 49
7. 24, 26
8. 58, 60
9. 28, 30

Page 45
2. 4 + 5 = 9
   5 + 4 = 9
   9 – 4 = 5
   9 – 5 = 4
3. 1 + 2 = 3
   2 + 1 = 3
   3 – 2 = 1
   3 – 1 = 2
4. 7 + 2 = 9
   2 + 7 = 9
   9 – 2 = 7
   9 – 7 = 2
5. 3 + 5 = 8
   5 + 3 = 8
   8 – 3 = 5
   8 – 5 = 3
6. 1 + 8 = 9
   8 + 1 = 9
   9 – 8 = 1
   9 – 1 = 8
7. 4 + 2 = 6
   2 + 4 = 6
   6 – 2 = 4
   6 – 4 = 2
8. 3 + 4 = 7
   4 + 3 = 7
   7 – 3 = 4
   7 – 4 = 3
9. 6 + 3 = 9
   3 + 6 = 9
   9 – 3 = 6
   9 – 6 = 3

Page 46
Check students answers. Any two items that equal 85¢ or less are acceptable.

Page 47
1. 14
2. 27
3. 32
4. 48
5. 58
6. 67
7. 100

Page 48
1. 2nd clock
2. 1st clock
3. 2nd clock
4. 2nd clock
5. 1st clock
6. 1st clock
7. 2nd clock
8. 1st clock

Page 49
Row 1: color boxes 2 & 3
Row 2: color box 3
Row 3: don't color anything
Row 4: color boxes 1 & 2
Row 5: color boxes 1 & 3

Page 50
2. 95, 59
3. 63, 36
4. 75, 57
5. 84, 48
6. 96, 69
7. 71, 17
8. 43, 34
9. 97, 79
10. 82, 28
11. 64, 46
12. 81, 18

Page 51
1. 5 + 10 = 15
2. 9 + 6 = 15
3. 10 + 2 = 12
4. 6 + 6 = 12
5. 14
6. 14
7. 11
8. 12
9. 11
10. 17
11. 15
12. 13
13. 16
14. 11

Page 52
50, 52, 54
40, 42, 43
31, 33, 34
21, 22, 24

Page 53
1. 7 candy bars
2. 11 cookies
3. 5 brownies
4. 13 candy wrappers
5. 10 chocolate chips
6. 2 more cupcakes

Page 54
1. $<$
2. $>$
3. $<$
4. =
5. $>$
6. $>$
7. $<$
8. =
9. $>$
10. =
11. $<$
12. $<$

Page 55
1. top clock
2. bottom clock
3. top clock
4. bottom clock
5. top clock
6. top clock
7. top clock
8. bottom clock

Page 56
1. 43, 41, 49
2. 19, 79, 9, 29
3. 25
4. 60, 30
5. 7, 8, 2
6. 100

Page 57
1. 1:00
2. 7:30
3. 1:30
4. 11:30
5. 8:00
6. 5:00
7. 10:00
8. 3:00
9. 4:30

Page 58
1. 952
2. 186
3. 403
4. 267
5. 398

Page 59
fifth – 5th
second – 2nd
first – 1st
seventh – 7th
tenth – 10th
third – 3rd
sixth – 6th
ninth – 9th
fourth – 4th
eighth – 8th

Page 60
1. Divide candy bar into 2 parts.
2. $\frac{1}{3}$
3. $\frac{1}{2}$
4. Divide sandwich into 2 parts.
5. Divide pizza into 4 parts.
6. Divide chocolate into 3 parts.

This Award Is Presented To

____

for

- ★ Doing Your Best
- ★ Trying Hard
- ★ Not Giving Up
- ★ Making a Great Effort